SPORTS SCIENCE

THE SCIENCE OF BASEBALL

NORMAN D. GRAUBART

PowerKiDS press

New York

Published in 2016 by The Rosen Publishing Group, Inc.
29 East 21st Street, New York, NY 10010

First Edition

Editor: Katie Kawa
Book Design: Katelyn Heinle

Photo Credits: Cover Will Hughes/Shutterstock.com; back cover kubais/Shutterstock.com; p. 5 Joy Brown/Shutterstock.com; p. 7 (baseball scene) colorcarnival/Shutterstock.com; p. 7 (radar gun) © iStockphoto.com/jpbcpa; p. 8 James Steidl/Shutterstock.com; p. 9 Sanit Fuangnakhon/Shutterstock.com; p. 11 (main) Rob Carr/Getty Images Sport/Getty Images; p. 11 (baseball interior) Edward Kinsman/Science Source/Getty Images; p. 13 Doug Pensinger/Getty Images Sport/Getty Images; p. 15 © iStockphoto.com/TerryJ; p. 17 Aspen Photo/Shutterstock.com; p. 19 Norm Hall/Getty Images Sport/Getty Images; p. 21 © iStockphoto.com/jgareri; p. 23 PETER MUHLY/AFP/Getty Images; p. 25 The Asahi Shimbun/Getty Images; p. 27 (left) Jamie Roach/Shutterstock.com; p. 27 (right) The Washington Post/Getty Images; p. 29 Eric Broder Van Dyke/Shutterstock.com; p. 30 Lothar Schulz/Getty Images.

Library of Congress Cataloging-in-Publication Data

Graubart, Norman D., author.
The science of baseball / Norman D. Graubart.
pages cm. — (Sports science)
Includes bibliographical references and index.
ISBN 978-1-4994-1063-1 (pbk.)
ISBN 978-1-4994-1099-0 (6 pack)
ISBN 978-1-4994-1122-5 (library binding)
1. Baseball—Juvenile literature. 2. Sports sciences—Juvenile literature. I. Title.
GV867.5.G6645 2016
796.357—dc23

2015008608

Manufactured in the United States of America

CPSIA Compliance Information: Batch #WS15PK: For Further Information contact Rosen Publishing, New York, New York at 1-800-237-9932

CONTENTS

A GAME OF HISTORY AND SCIENCE

Baseball is often called "America's game." Early forms of the sport were played as far back as the 1700s. **Professional** baseball has been around since the late 1860s, following the Civil War. Baseball is still one of America's most popular sports. Thousands of people go to ballparks to watch professional baseball games, and the sport is played on fields around the world.

What does baseball have to do with science? Science is everywhere! It helps us understand how the sport of baseball really works. It helps us understand why pitchers get tired, why some hits become game-winning home runs, and why catchers and other players use different gloves. This book will help you answer these questions and many more using fun science facts!

Baseball is one of America's most popular sports. Knowing the science behind the sport makes it even more fun to watch!

MIXING MATH AND SCIENCE

NUMBERS ARE A VERY IMPORTANT PART OF EVERY BASEBALL GAME, SO UNDERSTANDING MATH HELPS US BETTER UNDERSTAND BASEBALL. KNOWING HOW TO ADD, SUBTRACT, MULTIPLY, AND DIVIDE ALLOWS PEOPLE TO COMPARE BASEBALL PLAYERS IN A CLEAR WAY. MATH IS ALSO AN IMPORTANT PART OF PHYSICS, OR THE SCIENCE OF ENERGY AND HOW IT INTERACTS WITH MATTER. PHYSICS CAN BE SEEN IN ACTION DURING EVERY PLAY OF A BASEBALL GAME.

WHAT ARE STATS?

People have been keeping track of baseball players' and teams' statistics since professional baseball began. A statistic, or stat, is a number that stands for a piece of information. Stats are used in all sports to compare players and teams, but they're especially important in baseball because the game is filled with so many numbers. People who study stats are called statisticians or analysts. To be a baseball statistician, you have to be good at math.

Baseball statisticians figure out a lot of stats using percentages, or parts of a whole. Statisticians now use computers to help them find and compare baseball stats. However, it's still good to know how to use math on your own to compare the stats of your favorite baseball players.

RADAR GUNS

ONE OF THE MOST IMPORTANT NUMBERS IN ANY BASEBALL GAME IS THE SPEED OF EACH PITCH. THIS CAN BE MEASURED USING RADAR GUN TECHNOLOGY. RADAR GUNS WORK BY SHOOTING A BEAM OF **ELECTROMAGNETIC WAVES** AT A BASEBALL. THE WAVES THEN REFLECT, OR BOUNCE, BACK TO THE GUN AFTER HITTING THE BASEBALL, AND A SENSOR IN THE GUN USES THE REFLECTED WAVES TO MEASURE THE BALL'S SPEED.

EXTRA POINT

A special group called the Society for American Baseball Research (SABR) uses statistics and other kinds of math to study baseball.

Radar guns help statisticians compare different players' pitching speeds.

THE INFIELD AND ANGLES

Picture a baseball field from above. Look at the bases in the infield. They form a shape that's often called a baseball diamond, but it could also be called a baseball rhombus. A rhombus is a shape with four equal sides and opposite angles that are equal to one another.

A baseball diamond could have another name, too—a baseball square! A square is a special kind of rhombus with four equal sides and angles. All the lines between the bases on a baseball field are equal in length. Also, all the angles between these lines are 90 degrees. Angles that measure 90 degrees are known as right angles. A square is a shape with four right angles.

This is an example of a professional baseball infield. Many things about the game can change from **stadium** to stadium, but the dimensions and shape of the infield always stay the same.

EXTRA POINT

The dimensions of a softball infield are different from those of a baseball infield. There are 60 feet (18.3 m) between the bases on a softball field.

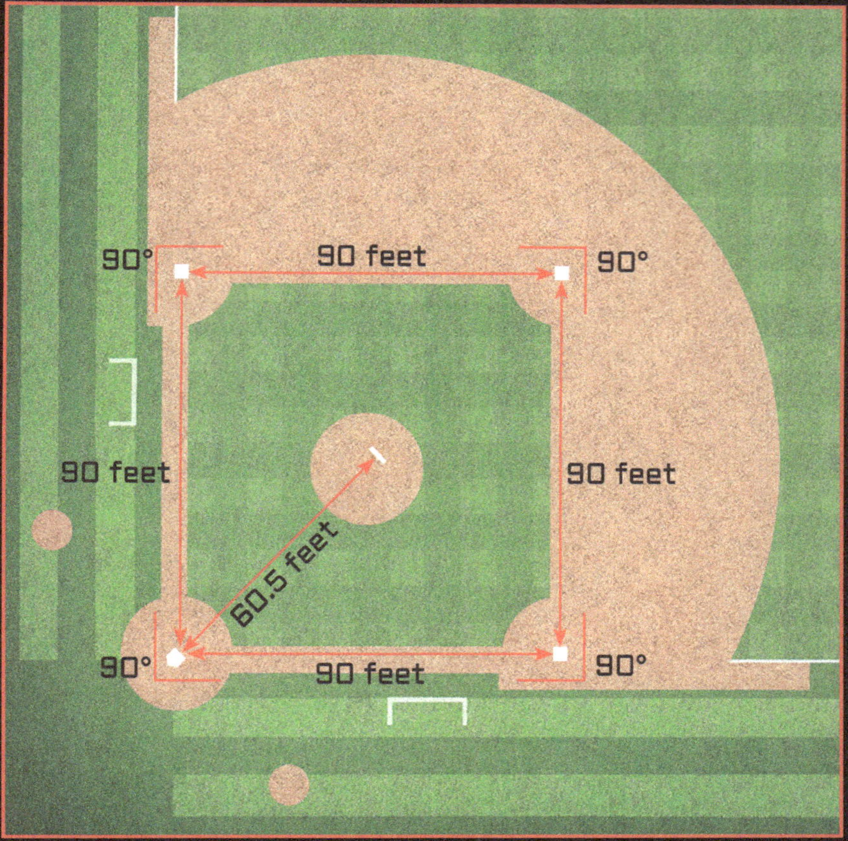

IDENTICAL INFIELDS

NO MATTER WHAT THE STADIUM MAY LOOK LIKE, ALL PROFESSIONAL BASEBALL INFIELDS HAVE THE SAME DIMENSIONS, OR MEASUREMENTS. THERE ARE ALWAYS 90 FEET (27.4 M) BETWEEN BASES, AND THERE ARE ALWAYS 60.5 FEET (18.4 M) BETWEEN THE PITCHER'S MOUND—SOMETIMES CALLED THE "RUBBER"—AND HOME PLATE.

BASEBALL AERODYNAMICS

Baseballs look like they're perfectly round. However, the red stitching on them makes it so they're not perfect spheres. The stitching actually affects how the ball is thrown and hit.

Pitchers are able to adjust the ball's movement using air resistance. Air is made of **molecules** like everything else. When a ball moves through the air, the air molecules push back on it. Pitchers throw the ball differently to allow different parts of the stitching to catch the air. Air flows differently around each area of the stitching, making the ball rise, curve, or drop unpredictably. A branch of science called aerodynamics studies the way air moves around objects, such as baseballs, and the way objects move through the air.

Pitchers are able to use air resistance, which is also called drag, to confuse hitters. Science helps them keep the other team from scoring!

ANATOMY OF A BASEBALL

HAVE YOU EVER WONDERED WHAT'S INSIDE A BASEBALL? AT THE CENTER IS A SMALL BALL OF CORK COVERED WITH RUBBER. THEN, SEVERAL KINDS OF YARN ARE WRAPPED AROUND THE CORK UNTIL THE BALL IS CLOSE TO THE SIZE OF THE FINAL BASEBALL. FINALLY, IT'S COVERED WITH LEATHER, AND THE RED STITCHING IS ADDED BY HAND.

EXTRA POINT

Baseballs made for the professional game commonly have 108 double stitches, or 216 total stitches.

CHANGES IN THE AIR

Air resistance can affect baseballs differently based on several factors. One factor is wind. If the wind is going in the same direction as a baseball, then it can push the ball farther. If the wind is pushing against the ball, though, the ball won't travel as far.

Air pressure also affects ball flight. Areas of high elevation have fewer air molecules than places closer to sea level. This means they have lower air pressure. One such place is Denver, Colorado. At Coors Field in Denver, which is where the Colorado Rockies play, it's easier to hit a home run than it is in almost every other baseball stadium. This is because there are fewer air molecules pushing on the ball and resisting its motion.

Coors Field is about 1 mile (1.6 km) above sea level, just like the rest of the city of Denver.

HUMIDITY HELPS

HUMIDITY, OR THE AMOUNT OF WATER IN THE AIR, ALSO AFFECTS HOW A BALL FLIES. WATER MOLECULES ARE LESS DENSE THAN OTHER MOLECULES IN THE AIR. THIS MEANS THAT HUMID AIR CREATES LESS AIR RESISTANCE ON THE BALL THAN DRY AIR. A BALL CAN TRAVEL LONGER DISTANCES IN HUMID AIR THAN IN DRY AIR IF EVERYTHING ELSE IS THE SAME.

EXTRA POINT

When baseball players play at higher elevations with lower air pressure, they might experience shortness of breath. This happens because lower air pressure means there's less oxygen in the air to breathe.

A FORCEFUL SWING

Baseball players use bats to hit the ball. The heavier the bat, the more mass it has. Mass is how much stuff there is in an object. Mass is like weight, but weight depends on **gravity**. A baseball bat might weigh 2 pounds (0.9 kg) on Earth, but it would weigh something else on another planet with a different amount of gravity. The bat's mass, however, will always be the same.

The more mass an object has, the more force is needed to put it in motion. A force is a push or pull on an object. Applied force is a force that one object applies to another. A baseball player swings their arms to apply force to the bat. The player needs to use more force to swing a bat with more mass.

PINE TAR

PROFESSIONAL BASEBALL PLAYERS SOMETIMES PUT PINE TAR ON THEIR BAT. PINE TAR IS STICKY, WHICH MEANS IT CAN HELP THE PLAYER GRIP THE BAT. PINE TAR CREATES MORE FRICTION BETWEEN A PLAYER'S HANDS AND THE WOODEN SURFACE OF A BAT. FRICTION IS A FORCE **EXERTED** WHEN ONE OBJECT MOVES ACROSS A SURFACE.

EXTRA POINT

The famous baseball player Babe Ruth sometimes used a bat that weighed over 2.5 pounds (1.1 kg). That's heavy for a baseball bat!

Heavier bats deliver a more powerful swing. However, they're harder to swing because more force is needed to move them.

BAT SPEED SCIENCE

A baseball player swings their bat with a circular motion. This motion can be measured in different ways. The first is speed. A batter's swing can be measured in miles or kilometers per hour, just like a pitch. The bat's movement can also be measured by its velocity. Velocity measures how fast an object changes its position. While a bat might have the same speed for most of the swing, its velocity is constantly changing.

EXTRA POINT

Another example of velocity is a baseball player running from one base to the next.

HIGH SPEED, LOW VELOCITY

WHEN A BASEBALL PLAYER HITS A HOME RUN, THEY RUN IN A CIRCLE AROUND THE BASES—STARTING AND ENDING AT HOME PLATE. EVEN IF THEY RUN QUICKLY, THEY END UP AT THE SAME PLACE AS THEIR STARTING POSITION, SO THEIR POSITION ULTIMATELY DIDN'T CHANGE. THIS MEANS THEY HAVE AN AVERAGE VELOCITY OF ZERO.

Velocity is an important measurement, because it tells scientists more about the movement of the object than speed alone. When an object, such as a bat being swung or ball being thrown, increases its velocity, it's said to be accelerating. Acceleration means a change in velocity, but it's most commonly used to describe an increase in velocity.

A swing can have a high speed but still have a velocity of zero. Even though the bat moved, it came back to its original place.

DIFFERENT GLOVES

All nine players on a baseball field wear a glove during the game. Most gloves have the same basic **design** except for the gloves worn by the first baseman and catcher. The first baseman's glove is larger than most. Why is this? The larger glove gives the first baseman more surface area to catch the ball. This is useful for times when ground balls are hit to other infielders, and they have to throw quickly to first base. The larger glove helps first basemen reach balls that aren't thrown perfectly.

These larger gloves have more mass, though, which means it's harder to move them quickly. While more surface area is helpful for first basemen, quick movement is more important for many other players. This is why players at other positions use smaller gloves with less mass.

A glove's surface area is more important to a first baseman than most other baseball players because first basemen get more balls thrown to them from all over the field. They need a glove that will give them the best chance of making tough catches.

PITCHERS' GLOVES

PITCHERS' GLOVES ARE ALSO DIFFERENT FROM BASIC GLOVES. WHILE MANY GLOVES HAVE A WEBBED POCKET WITH SMALL HOLES FOR THE BALL TO REST IN, PITCHERS' GLOVES DON'T. PITCHERS DON'T WANT THE BATTERS TO SEE WHAT KIND OF GRIP THEY HAVE ON THE BALL, WHICH WOULD LET THE BATTER KNOW WHAT KIND OF PITCH IS COMING.

EXTRA POINT

Baseball gloves are made of leather. Players warm and soften the leather to make their glove more **flexible**.

MOTION AND MITTS

Catchers also use different gloves, which are sometimes called mitts. Catchers' mitts need to have a lot of padding. The edge of a catcher's mitt is thick, which helps catchers trap the ball after it hits their palm.

Catchers' mitts need to be thick because of how hard pitchers throw. The harder the ball hits the catcher's mitt, the greater the amount of force a catcher uses to stop it. This is because of Isaac Newton's third law of motion, which states that for every action, there's an equal and opposite **reaction**. The thickness of the mitt helps **protect** a catcher's hand from the force of the pitch.

ISAAC NEWTON

ISAAC NEWTON WAS AN ENGLISH SCIENTIST WHO LIVED FROM 1643 TO 1727. HE'S OFTEN CONSIDERED THE FATHER OF MODERN PHYSICS. NEWTON USED SCIENCE AND MATH TO STUDY THE WORLD AROUND HIM IN A WAY NO ONE HAD BEFORE. HIS THREE LAWS OF MOTION DESCRIBE THE RELATIONSHIP BETWEEN FORCES ACTING ON AN OBJECT AND THE OBJECT'S MOTION.

EXTRA POINT

Catchers wear a lot of gear to protect their body from the force of the pitches thrown at them. Their gear includes a mask, chest protector, and shin guards.

law	What does it mean?	baseball example
Newton's first law	An object at rest stays at rest and an object in motion stays in motion with the same speed and direction unless acted on by an outside force.	A baseball resting on the ground will stay there until a player picks it up to throw it.
Newton's second law	The greater the mass of an object, the greater the force needed to make the object accelerate.	A person needs to use more force to swing a baseball bat with more mass than a bat with less mass.
Newton's third law	For every action, there's an equal and opposite reaction.	When a ball hits a bat, it bounces off the bat with an equal amount of force.

Although Newton lived hundreds of years ago, his three laws of motion still apply to the world around us today.

HOW FAR WILL IT GO?

Newton's third law of motion is also important if you want to understand hitting. Imagine that two batters swing their bats at the same speed, and they hit two baseballs with the same part of the bat. The first batter hits a fastball that's going 90 miles (144.8 km) per hour. The next batter hits a pitch that's traveling 75 miles (120.7 km) per hour. Which ball will go farther?

EXTRA POINT

The spin of the ball in the air can also affect its speed and direction when it hits the bat.

PLAYING THE ANGLES

THE ANGLE AT WHICH A PLAYER HOLDS THEIR BAT PLAYS A PART IN WHERE THE BALL WILL GO AFTER IT'S HIT. NO TWO PLAYERS HOLD THEIR BAT IN EXACTLY THE SAME WAY, SO THEY EACH CREATE A DIFFERENT ANGLE BETWEEN THE BAT AND THE PITCH'S TRAJECTORY, OR PATH IN THE AIR.

The ball that was going faster will go farther. That ball hits the bat with more force, so it will bounce off the bat with more force, too. The force of the reaction must be equal to the force of the original action. If both hitters have the same bat speed, then the one who hits a faster pitch will hit the ball farther.

Baseball players work hard to find the right bat angle and amount of force to turn pitches into home runs.

AN ENERGETIC SPORT

Pitching is a good example of the difference between potential energy and kinetic energy. Potential energy is the amount of energy stored by an object when the object isn't using the energy. Kinetic energy is the energy that the object is using to do work. When a pitcher holds the ball before a pitch, the ball has potential energy because it's not in motion. Once the ball is released, it has kinetic energy because it's moving toward the batter.

There are many other examples of potential and kinetic energy in baseball. When a player holds their bat high up before they swing it, the bat has potential energy. The swing changes the potential energy to kinetic energy.

HUMAN ENERGY

ENERGY IS ALSO IMPORTANT FOR YOUR BODY. HUMANS DON'T HAVE AN UNLIMITED SUPPLY OF ENERGY. THIS IS WHY STARTING PITCHERS OFTEN LEAVE THE GAME AFTER SEVERAL INNINGS. THEY USE A LOT OF ENERGY TO THROW THE BALL AS HARD AS THEY CAN. THEN, A RELIEF OR CLOSING PITCHER WILL THROW THE BALL VERY HARD FOR ONE OR TWO INNINGS.

This chart shows more examples of potential and kinetic energy at a baseball game.

examples of potential energy	examples of kinetic energy
a player standing still on a base	a player running from one base to another
a baseball resting in a player's glove	a baseball being thrown from one player to another
fans sitting still in their seats	fans jumping up to cheer after a home run

EXTRA POINT

Energy can neither be created nor destroyed. It can only change forms. This is known as the law of **conservation** of energy.

During a baseball game, you'll sometimes see a player run through first base without stopping after a hit. First base is the only base a player can run past without having to worry about being called out. This is because it's hard for baseball players to stop on first base as soon as they reach it due to their momentum.

Momentum is the quantity, or amount, of motion an object has. It can be found by multiplying an object's mass by its velocity. The more momentum an object has, the harder it is to stop its motion. Professional baseball players generally have a lot of mass because they're big, strong athletes. They're also moving at a high velocity from home plate to first base, so they can make it to the base without slowing down. This means their momentum is great, and it carries them through first base.

Momentum makes it hard for a base runner to stop running once they get started.

LET IT SLIDE

SOMETIMES PLAYERS NEED TO SLIDE TO REACH A BASE WITHOUT BEING CALLED OUT. WHEN BASEBALL PLAYERS SLIDE INTO A BASE, THEY DON'T HAVE TO SLOW DOWN AS MUCH AS THEY DO WHEN THEY'RE RUNNING UPRIGHT. THEY CAN SLIDE WITH ENOUGH MOMENTUM TO REACH THE BASE SAFELY. THIS IS WHY MANY PLAYERS PREFER TO SLIDE INTO A BASE WHEN THEY NEED TO MAKE IT THERE QUICKLY.

EXTRA POINT

An object at rest always has a momentum of zero because its mass isn't in motion.

SLIPPERY SPITBALLS

Pitchers know how to change their grip on the ball to make it harder for batters to hit their pitches. Some illegal pitches make the ball even harder to hit. One of them is the spitball. A spitball is any baseball that has spit or some other liquid on some part of the ball. The liquid changes the ball's aerodynamics and makes it move unevenly.

The slippery surface of a spitball makes the ball come out of the pitcher's hand more easily. This is because the liquid reduces friction between the pitcher's hand and the ball. Spitballs and other pitches that involve doctoring, or altering, the ball were banned from professional baseball in 1920.

Science can be used to help players improve their skills as they play by the rules. Unfortunately, science has also been used to help players find ways to break those rules.

THE STEROID ERA

STEROIDS, WHICH ARE CHEMICAL **SUBSTANCES** USED TO HELP PEOPLE GET BIGGER AND STRONGER, ARE A BIG PROBLEM IN MANY SPORTS, INCLUDING BASEBALL. MANY PLAYERS WHO SET HOME RUN RECORDS DURING THE LATE 1990S AND EARLY 2000S ADMITTED TO USING STEROIDS, WHICH ARE BANNED SUBSTANCES IN BASEBALL. THE LATEST TECHNOLOGY IS USED BY PROFESSIONAL BASEBALL OFFICIALS TO TEST FOR STEROIDS IN THE BODIES OF BASEBALL PLAYERS.

EXTRA POINT

A substance used to reduce friction, such as the spit on a spitball, is known as a lubricant.

SCIENCE, BASEBALL, AND YOU

When you're in the middle of a baseball game, it might be hard to think about how science is affecting the game. However, it's helpful to remember how to keep science on your side as you play.

If you want to get to the next base quickly, use your momentum to slide. If you're a catcher and the pitcher throws the ball with a lot of force, make sure your mitt is able to help lessen the impact. Finally, if you want to be a home-run hitter, your best chance is to play for the Colorado Rockies.

The next time you watch a baseball game, pay attention to the physics on the field. It's fun to see science in action at the ballpark!

GLOSSARY

air pressure: The force exerted by air molecules.

conservation: The act of keeping a constant amount of something during a process of change.

design: A plan for how something should look.

electromagnetic waves: Waves that carry energy. Examples of electromagnetic waves include visible light, radio waves, and X-rays.

exert: To put forth.

flexible: Capable of bending easily.

gravity: The natural force that pulls objects toward the center of Earth, another planet, or a star.

molecule: The smallest part of something.

professional: Having to do with a job someone does for a living.

protect: To keep safe.

reaction: The force that an object subjected to an outside force exerts in the opposite direction.

stadium: A large, commonly outdoor building where people gather to watch sporting events.

substance: Matter of a certain kind.

INDEX

WEBSITES

Due to the changing nature of Internet links, PowerKids Press has developed an online list of websites related to the subject of this book. This site is updated regularly. Please use this link to access the list: www.powerkidslinks.com/spsci/base